BLACK TRAILBLAZERS IN SPORTS

DOUG WILLIAMS

by David Lee Morgan Jr.

FOCUS READERS®
NAVIGATOR

WWW.FOCUSREADERS.COM

Focus Readers is distributed by North Star Editions:
sales@northstareditions.com | 888-417-0195

Produced for Focus Readers by Red Line Editorial.

Photographs ©: Paul Spinelli/NFL Photos/AP Images, cover, 1; Bud Symes/Getty Images Sport/Getty Images, 4–5; Stephen Dunn/Getty Images Sport/Getty Images, 6; Bettmann/Getty Images, 9; Joan Sydlow/FPG/Hulton Archive/Archive Photos/Getty Images, 10–11; AP Images, 13, 15; Focus on Sport/Getty Images Sport/Getty Images, 16–17, 18; Mike Powell/Getty Images Sport/Getty Images, 21; Stephen Dunn/Allsport/Hulton Archive/Getty Images, 22–23; Bill Haber/AP Images, 25; Kevin Mazur/Roc Nation/Getty Images Entertainment/Getty Images, 27; Red Line Editorial, 29

Library of Congress Cataloging-in-Publication Data
Names: Morgan, David Lee, author.
Title: Doug Williams / by David Lee Morgan Jr.
Description: Mendota Heights, MN: Focus Readers, [2025] | Series: Black trailblazers in sports | Includes bibliographical references and index. | Audience: Grades 4-6
Identifiers: LCCN 2024001394 (print) | LCCN 2024001395 (ebook) | ISBN 9798889982142 (hardcover) | ISBN 9798889982708 (paperback) | ISBN 9798889983774 (pdf) | ISBN 9798889983262 (ebook)
Subjects: LCSH: Williams, Doug, 1955---Juvenile literature. | Quarterbacks (Football)--United States--Biography--Juvenile literature. | African American football players--Biography--Juvenile literature.
Classification: LCC GV939.W49 M67 2025 (print) | LCC GV939.W49 (ebook) | DDC 796.332/092 [B]--dc20/eng/20240122
LC record available at https://lccn.loc.gov/2024001394
LC ebook record available at https://lccn.loc.gov/2024001395

Printed in the United States of America
Mankato, MN
082024

ABOUT THE AUTHOR

David Lee Morgan Jr. is the author of 11 books, including *LeBron James: The Rise of a Star* and *Breaking Through the Lines: The Marion Motley Story*. Morgan was a longtime sportswriter with the *Akron Beacon Journal* and is now a high school English teacher and public speaker.

TABLE OF CONTENTS

17
REDSKINS
17

CHAPTER 1

SUPER BOWL HISTORY

No one expected Doug Williams to become a Super Bowl star. He began the 1987 season as Washington's backup quarterback. But now, in January 1988, he was the team's starter. And he was playing on the biggest stage in the National Football League (NFL). Williams was also making history. He had become

Washington quarterback Doug Williams passes during the Super Bowl in January 1988.

Williams completed 18 passes during the Super Bowl.

the first Black quarterback to start in the Super Bowl.

Washington faced the Denver Broncos. The Broncos scored on their first offensive play. Broncos quarterback John Elway launched a long pass. Wide receiver Ricky Nattiel caught it for a touchdown. Later in the first quarter, the Broncos kicked a field goal. That put Washington down 10–0. Denver looked completely in control.

However, Williams took over in the second quarter. First, he found Ricky Sanders, who scored on an 80-yard touchdown play. On Washington's next drive, Williams passed to Gary Clark for a 27-yard touchdown. Later in the second quarter, Sanders caught another touchdown pass from Williams. Then, near the end of the quarter, Williams tossed a touchdown pass to Clint Didier. Williams had just thrown four touchdown passes in the second quarter. He set a Super Bowl record for the most in one quarter.

By halftime, Washington led 35–10. The team never looked back. Washington won the game 42–10. Williams had passed for 340 yards. At the time, that was a Super Bowl record.

After the game, the announcer spoke to the crowd. He told the fans that Doug Williams was the game's Most Valuable Player (MVP). That meant Williams had made even more history. He became the first Black quarterback to earn the Super Bowl MVP Award. The crowd erupted with a standing ovation.

Williams celebrates after winning the Super Bowl.

Some fans believe Williams had the greatest Super Bowl performance of all time. Former Washington quarterback Joe Theismann agreed. He had won a Super Bowl in the 1982 season. Theismann said Williams's performance was what dreams are made of.

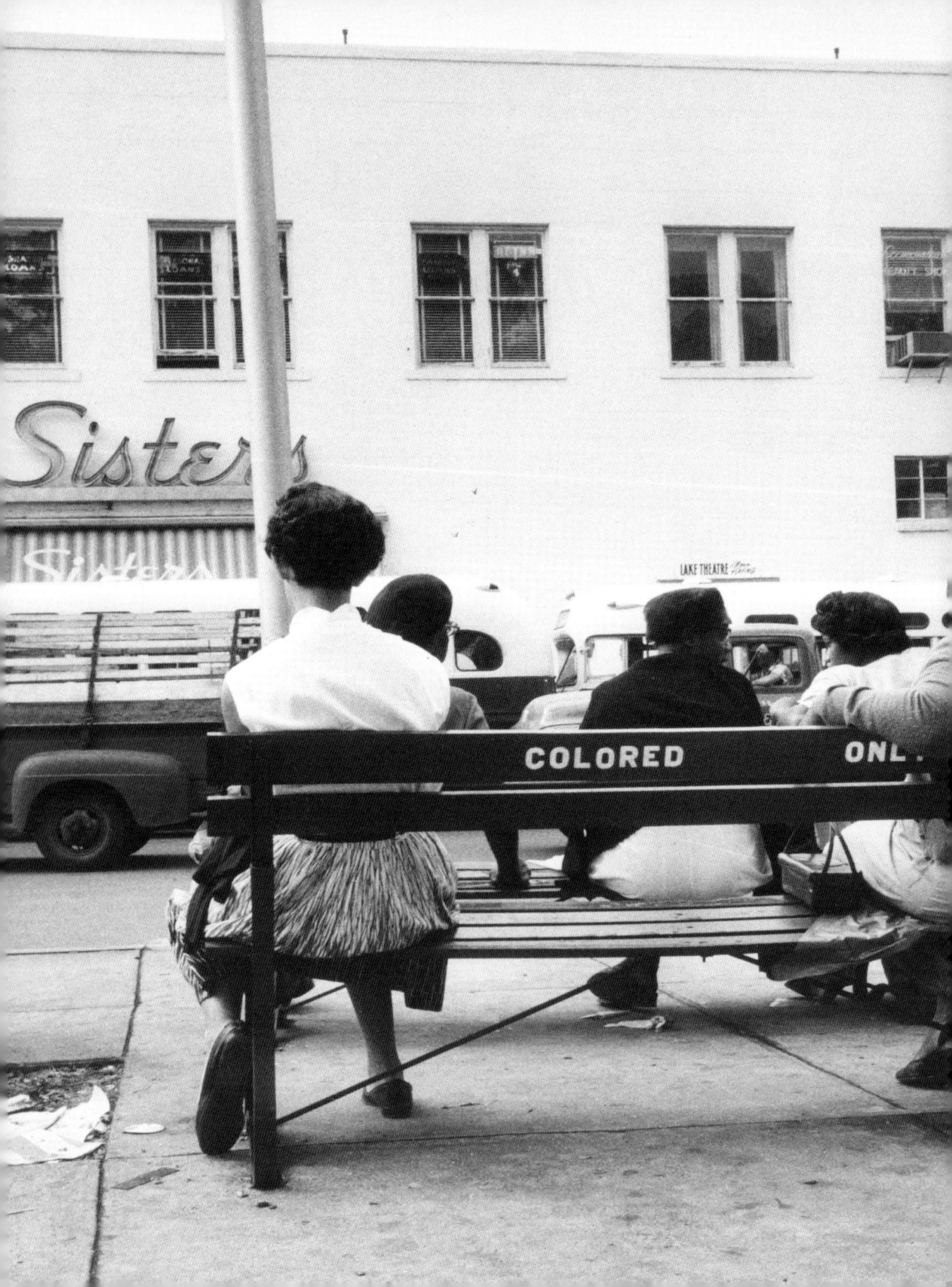

Sisters
LAKE THEATRE
COLORED

CHAPTER 2

YOUNG SUPERSTAR

Doug Williams was born on August 9, 1955, in Zachary, Louisiana. He was the sixth of eight children. His family lived in a **segregated** area. Racist laws denied Black Americans good jobs. Laws also kept Black people from certain public places. And the laws prevented Black people from voting.

Segregation laws kept white and Black people separate. Facilities for Black people were often much worse.

Doug grew up during the **civil rights movement**. Across the United States, Black Americans protested against racist systems. At the same time, racist groups worked to keep those systems in place. One group was the Ku Klux Klan. It used terror and violence. Doug saw this terror when he was 10 years old. The Klan regularly burned crosses near his house.

Doug faced some violence directly. One day, he was walking to the store. Then, someone in a passing car threw a milkshake at him. It hit Doug while he was walking. Doug actually felt lucky. The object could have been something more dangerous.

Williams (12) looks for an open Grambling State teammate during a 1977 game.

Doug developed a passion for football. He became a star quarterback in high school. Even so, major colleges did not show much interest in him. In response, Doug chose to play at Grambling State University.

Williams started in all four years of college. He helped make the Grambling State Tigers great. Williams could throw the long ball with a perfect spiral. He recorded 93 touchdown passes as a Tiger. That set an **NCAA** record. Williams was named Black College Player of the

HBCUs

Grambling State University is an HBCU. HBCUs are historically Black colleges and universities. The first HBCUs opened during the mid-1800s. At the time, most colleges and universities did not allow Black students. This was racist **discrimination.** HBCUs were a powerful response. They provided higher education to Black Americans. There are approximately 100 HBCUs still open today.

Williams threw for 8,411 yards in his four years as Grambling State's quarterback.

Year twice. Grambling State also won three **conference** championships.

In 1977, Williams finished fourth in the Heisman Trophy voting. This award goes to the season's best college football player. He finished college the next year. Williams was clearly ready for the next level.

CHAPTER 3

BREAKING BARRIERS

The Tampa Bay Buccaneers selected Doug Williams in the 1978 draft. He was picked 17th overall. That made history. He became the first Black quarterback drafted in the first round.

Williams joined Tampa Bay as the team was starting its third season ever. The Buccaneers had won only two games in

In 1978, Williams came in third for the NFL's Rookie of the Year Award.

Williams was named the Buccaneers' MVP in both 1980 and 1981.

their first two years. Williams changed that. In his first season, the Buccaneers won five games.

The next season was even better. The Buccaneers went 10–6 in the regular season. Then Williams took them to the conference championship game. He showed he was a top NFL quarterback.

Williams also proved he was as **clutch** as they come. He had four game-winning drives in 1980. That was the most in the NFL. He led the league in game-winning drives again in 1981. He also took Tampa Bay back to the playoffs that season.

BLACK QUARTERBACKS

In the 1970s, all the NFL's owners and head coaches were white. Many of them believed racist **stereotypes**. They believed Black people were less intelligent than white people. This is completely false. But many white owners and coaches thought Black players couldn't succeed at quarterback. That's because the position requires a lot of intelligence. Williams's success helped prove the stereotype wrong.

After the 1982 season, Williams and the team's owner had a disagreement. It was about money. Williams was one of the lowest-paid quarterbacks in the league. He felt he should earn more. But the owner didn't budge. So, Williams decided to sit out the 1983 season.

In 1984, Williams joined a new league. It was called the United States Football League (USFL). That year, Williams passed for 3,084 yards and 15 touchdowns. Williams played even better the next year. But after the 1985 season, the USFL shut down.

In 1986, Williams returned to the NFL. Washington needed a backup

In January 1988, Washington defeated the Minnesota Vikings in the playoffs to advance to the Super Bowl.

quarterback, so the team signed him. But Washington's starter struggled during the 1987 season. Williams took over. He led his team through the playoffs. Then he became the first Black quarterback to win the Super Bowl.

Riddell
17
53

CHAPTER 4

BLACK ROYALTY

Doug Williams started for Washington in the 1988 season. However, injuries and surgeries slowed him down. By the end of the season, he was a backup. Williams remained with Washington in 1989. But after the season, the team let him go. Williams hoped to join another team, but no one would sign him. He

Williams played just four games for Washington in 1989.

believed it was because he was Black. He decided to retire from the NFL.

Williams stayed in football, though. In 1991, he began coaching. He became the head coach at a high school in Louisiana.

Over the years, Williams worked his way up the coaching ladder. In 1994, he landed a job as an assistant coach for a college. Three years later, he got his first college head coaching position. The job was at Morehouse College in Atlanta, Georgia. Like Grambling State, Morehouse is an HBCU. Williams coached at Morehouse for a year. Then he got the head coaching job at his old college, Grambling State.

Williams's overall record as coach of Grambling State was 52–18.

In 2004, Williams returned to the NFL. He stuck to his old teams. He worked as an **executive** for the Tampa Bay Buccaneers. Then, in 2014, he became an executive with Washington. He made important decisions for the team. He became the top adviser to the team's president in 2021.

Williams has been an inspiration for many Black players. He showed that Black quarterbacks were just as smart

PAVING THE WAY

For years, Williams was the only Black quarterback with a Super Bowl ring. That finally changed in the 2013 season. Russell Wilson led the Seattle Seahawks to a title. Six years later, Patrick Mahomes became the third Black quarterback to win the big game. Mahomes led the Kansas City Chiefs to another title in the 2022 season. That game made even more history. Mahomes faced Jalen Hurts of the Philadelphia Eagles. It was the first Super Bowl with two Black starting quarterbacks.

In the 2022 NFL season, Williams shows off the Lombardi Trophy before the Super Bowl.

and talented as white quarterbacks. Williams accomplished great things on and off the field. That is why many people call him Black royalty.

DOUG WILLIAMS

- **Height:** 6 feet 4 inches (193 cm)
- **Weight:** 220 pounds (100 kg)
- **Born:** August 9, 1955
- **Birthplace:** Zachary, Louisiana
- **High school:** Chaneyville (Zachary, Louisiana)
- **College:** Grambling State University (Grambling, Louisiana) (1974–77)
- **Major achievements:** NCAA All-American (1977); Black College Player of the Year (1976–77); Super Bowl champion (1987); Super Bowl MVP (1987)

Washington, DC
Atlanta
Grambling
Zachary
Tampa

FOCUS ON

DOUG WILLIAMS

Write your answers on a separate piece of paper.

1. Write a paragraph explaining the main ideas of Chapter 3.
2. Why do you think it took so long for a Black starting quarterback to appear in the Super Bowl?
3. Which NFL team drafted Doug Williams?
    A. Tampa Bay
    B. Denver
    C. Washington
4. How did Williams's game-winning drives show that he was clutch?
    A. Williams didn't play any differently at the beginnings or ends of games.
    B. Williams played better when his team was way ahead.
    C. Williams succeeded on the last chances to win games.

Answer key on page 32.

GLOSSARY

civil rights movement

A mass struggle against racial discrimination in the United States in the 1950s and 1960s.

clutch

Having to do with a difficult situation when the outcome of the game is in question.

conference

A group of teams within a league.

discrimination

Unfair treatment of others based on who they are or how they look.

executive

A powerful person in a business who makes important decisions.

NCAA

Short for National Collegiate Athletic Association, a college sports organization in the United States.

segregated

Separate or set apart based on race, gender, or religion.

stereotypes

Oversimplified, unfair, or untrue ideas about what all members of a certain group are like.

TO LEARN MORE

BOOKS

Coleman, Ted. *Tampa Bay Buccaneers All-Time Greats.* Mendota Heights, MN: Press Box Books, 2022.

Goodman, Michael E. *Washington Commanders.* Mankato, MN: Creative Education, 2023.

Wing, Kelisa. *Historically Black Colleges and Universities.* Ann Arbor, MI: Cherry Lake Publishing, 2022.

NOTES TO EDUCATORS

Visit **www.focusreaders.com** to find lesson plans, activities, links, and other resources related to this title.

INDEX

Answer Key: 1. Answers will vary; **2.** Answers will vary; **3.** A; **4.** C